CW00524692

Kulvinder Kherteru is a _____-law, a wife and a mother. She has always _____ _____ion for reading books since childhood. In her late 40s, she obtained her GCSE in English within six months and completed her BA Honour's degree over the period of eight years. She has been working in Special Needs Education for 19 years to date and continues to do so.

To my children, Rajan and Karam.

Kulvinder Kherteru

A Small Creation of Literature

Short Stories and Poems

AUSTIN MACAULEY PUBLISHERS™

LONDON • CAMBRIDGE • NEW YORK • SHARJAH

Copyright © Kulvinder Kherteru (2019)

The right of Kulvinder Kherteru to be identified as author of this work has been asserted by her in accordance with section 77 and 78 of the Copyright, Designs and Patents Act 1988.

All rights reserved. No part of this publication may be reproduced, stored in a retrieval system or transmitted in any form or by any means, electronic, mechanical, photocopying, recording or otherwise, without the prior permission of the publishers.

Any person who commits any unauthorised act in relation to this publication may be liable to criminal prosecution and civil claims for damages.

A CIP catalogue record for this title is available from the British Library.

ISBN 9781528923477 (Paperback)
ISBN 9781528964173 (ePub e-book)

www.austinmacauley.com

First Published (2019)
Austin Macauley Publishers Ltd
25 Canada Square
Canary Wharf
London
E14 5LQ

My father-in-law and mother-in-law for not letting me give up when I had had enough. Thanking them for their ongoing support, always. For everyone else who had helped me to complete my degree whether it was a small or a big contribution. Thank you.

A Bunch of Flowers

I sat in my chair staring out of the window, it was a sunny day. My body just sank into the soft chair and my mind wondered back to that dreadful day. The events had taken place after my husband had passed on. We had a beautiful home, two lovely boys, life was bliss. My husband owned a business, and I was a good history teacher. My eldest son had left home and made his own way in life joining the military and succeeding in his job. My youngest son, now 22, had a lot of issues. I mean we tried, my husband and I to talk to him, support him and to love him, he did not make it easy for us. Under our close supervision he had somewhat escaped into a different world, a world of drugs.

'You never did anything for me, never,' Paul would shout at the top of his voice. The changes soon came; Paul would stay out all night; his room would smell of 'plants' all the time.

'We need to get you professional help Paul, listen to us,' Craig, my husband, would say. It got very bad to a point where money would go missing; Paul lost the will to live. He was a very handsome boy and had potential to do well but the drugs took a toll on him. He lost his weight, became very frail; his skin was pale and taunt. I always kept his nails short and black-dirt free; now, they were long and dirty, so was he, dirty. His emotional outbursts, the shouting matches between us and the long endless nights that we had to keep guard, soon affected us. My husband would say, 'Jean, we cannot go on like this; we are all suffering.' What could I do? My precious boy. I just wanted to keep him close to me, always.

My world nearly fell apart when Craig had gone but I knew I had to be brave for Paul. But things got worse, not better. I really tried but I just could not reach him; he had gone out too far. Three months on and the shouting matches started, it was all too much. I was alone; I couldn't cope, and I couldn't handle him. 'Paul I love you, you have to stop this,' I said.

'I never want to see you again,' he said then he walked out. I was devastated.

Two years passed, I did not hear from Paul but I did not give up. Hope and faith took me from one day to another. I retired from my job, sold my house and went into an "elderly nursing home". The years had been kind to me but old age catches up on us all. My older son, Eric, would often visit and reminisce about the past. He did not hear from Paul either.

The bunch of flowers was beautiful, they had brought with them a new day, a vision of the future. The roses were bright and alive and the room seems to come to life with their presence. They had arrived this morning just after breakfast and had been placed on my side table in my room. I stared at the bunch of flowers. I felt alive; I felt happy and cried at the same time. Words cannot describe the life I once knew, the destruction of my family that I had suffered, and now this bunch of flowers had brought the love back into my life. The accompanying card simply read, 'I love you, Mother. Please forgive me,' signed your son Paul.

Answering Back

The beautiful sun was bright and sharp and its rays fell all around. It shone on all the houses and pavements and made the roads look clean. In the background, the distant factories surrounded the area. It had constant smoke coming out of their chimneys and it was not long before the sun became dull. The noise of children laughing, crying and parents talking was apparent but the house in the middle of the street fell silent. This house was quite old but to look at it also new in some places. The worn out bricks once showed their redness of the inner brick were now a deep brown. The ivy just made its way up to the roof over the years and clambered on to the house like a net with no chance of other flowers blossoming. The windows are quite big but the drawn black curtains made them look smaller. The battered white door, displayed imprinted black marks that remained forever embedded and the motive for cleaning them was forgotten. There were eight concrete slabs that led up to the rusty gate. There were gaps between the houses on this street but the clean look and the warmth that came across as you passed each house had skipped this one.

    David appeared at the door and he quietly shut it and then he ran up the path. He looked like he was in a rush and he was, he was late for school. His hair was long and swayed side to side; as he ran, this made his face visible, it was a grubby face. He was very thin but looked quite strong. The black flare trousers he wore had two faint holes appearing at the knees and the dirty grey shirt, once white, was not tucked in. He had no coat. He sprinted over the gate and onto the pavement. 'W-wait for me, I have f-finished all m-my chores,' Kenny said as he came out of the house slamming the door behind him;

he stumbled clumsily across the path over to the gate. He was tall but more built. The clothes he wore were identical to David's but the only difference was Kenny had a scruffy light burgundy jacket on. It was not just the hair or the whole attire, David and Kenny were twin brothers. The only difference was that Kenny was the younger brother who spoke with a stammer.

'Shush…' said David, 'Quiet, she will hear us.'

Both the boys fell silent as they scurried side by side up the road.

The loud bell made a din; both the boys had just made it. The day just floated past and the home time bell just seems to toll and toll.

'Hurry up,' said David,

'I am c-coming, wait,' came the reply.

'I said, hurry up before,' David continued, his voice was full of concern. It was too late; both the boys found them pushed against the wall. There were four of them, taller and bigger. 'Well, well, if it isn't the scruffiest brothers in school, what is the matter your mother can't afford new clothes? Just look at them, how dirty,' the voice was menacing and the sound deafening.

The brothers just stood with their heads hanging in shame, their shoulders slumped and their hands by their sides. The brothers had given up; they were tired of it all and just waited for the outcome that they were familiar with.

A rather large boy grabbed the collar of the burgundy jacket and nearly uprooted Kenny of the floor. This bully was a big boy, heavy on the shoulders, you know the type he could easily become a rugby player. His uniform was immaculate, not a dust of dirt insight, not even on the white collar. His hands were huge and his fingers were like fat sausages. Even though he was smart to look at, his bullying made him very ugly. David dared not to look up but after the fourth punch, he fell to the ground. Kenny soon fell, following his older sibling down onto the pavement.

'H-help us,' he said, reaching his hand out to the boys as if he wanted the bullies to help them in their crisis, not in the bullying they were receiving but his words fell on deaf ears. The bullies did not hear the real cry of the pain the one that came from inside nor did they see the suffering in their eyes. The verbal abuse from the bigger boys could be still heard in the distance. Both the brothers were silent as they walked home.

They looked for something to eat, there was nothing as usual and they were quite used to it. The empty vodka bottle lay rolling on the floor. 'Don't make a sound, just go up,' David whispered. Kenny slowly sneaked up the stairs, the creaking noise became louder. They both got to the top and let out a sigh of relief. As they turned to go into the bedroom, David disappeared. It was all very sudden as he didn't see his drunken mother crawling up the stairs behind them. She had grabbed David from his hair and dragged him back down.

'Good for nothing, school, what is school? What about my jobs?' she snarled.

Her eyes were very red and you could smell the vodka each time she opened her mouth. She was in her late 50s, the wrinkles on her face could be seen clearly; she was of a medium build but was not in the right frame of mind to either stand or speak. Her washed-out green bathrobe was now a murky grey colour, and she had one slipper on and one off. Her hand came down hard across her eldest son's face, and he nearly fell again.

Kenny came running down the stairs, 'M-m-mother no!' he struggled as he spoke.

'Stop right there,' his mother snapped. Her arm was stretched out and her hand pointed at him. He froze in fear. 'Fighting again, has you? What do you think this is? Perhaps you need to be taught a lesson,' she shouted. 'Just like you're good for nothing father, where is he? Where is he?' she shouted, again and again.

David was quite shaken; he already had a beating earlier on but this was no surprise either.

'Please, Mother. What is it that you want?' he asked, not even looking up.

'Where's my bottle? Which one of you little bastards has stolen it?' she screamed.

She dragged her eldest by his hair right up to the settee and plonked him next to her. Her second son had only managed to get down one step; he was too scared to go any further.

'If I don't get my bottle, you know what is going to happen. Well, let me tell you,' she said. She continued to blame, fault and repeat herself; she wallowed in self-pity at the same time.

Their father had left a long time ago. The brothers could not remember his face, and there were no pictures of him at all in the house but one. This was no good as the face had been burnt out with a cigarette burn and the chances of ever finding him again had gone. The more she spoke, the more she started to drift off. She would open her eyes in-between and demand to know where she was. Two hours had past, but it seemed like forever. She finally fell asleep, letting go of the firstborn.

'Come q-quickly,' Kenny called out, who was still standing on the stairs; his legs were cold and stiff. They both climbed up the stairs as if there was light at the end of them. Kenny managed to push the heavy old chair in front of the door. They locked the door and then they both fell on the cardboard boxes on the floor. Their bodies ached with the pain but they arose from it like it was, well, normal, just like every other day. No more voices, just silence.

There was no sun the next morning, just rain. By the time they had got to school, both the brothers were tired. They were also hungry and wet. The hustle and bustle of the school day seemed to just float passed them again. They were called into the office. Mrs Turner was the prettiest teacher there but she was on a mission.

'Is everything okay boys? I mean are you two okay? How is your mother?' she asked in a concerned voice. The boys had remembered very well how smart their mother was when she had to come into school one time. She had laughed to Mrs Turner about the appearance of her sons as, 'You know what boys are like, always getting dirty while playing, that's all they think about; why sometimes they even forget to eat,' she had assured the nosey teacher.

Kenny struggled to speak.

'M-Mrs. T-Turner,' he whispered, but his brother just looked at him, he knew then that there was no point and no way out.

'Yes, we are fine, Mrs Turner,' David answered with a smile.

'Only if there is anything you want to talk about, any concerns; we are always here to listen and help you,' came the reply.

'Yes and thank you,' David ended the conversation quickly as he knew very well that his life would not be worth living if they continued any further.

They looked over their shoulders as they tried to get out of school, it was no use. Kenny got caught straight away so David had no choice but to follow. They were taken to the park around the corner just by the pond.

'Why don't you have a bath? We think you both need one,' one of the bullies shouted. It started to rain even harder, they were drenched as it was, and they had nothing to lose. The biggest and the ugliest bully came forward again and pushed David into the pond after twisting his arms hard; he had landed in the shallow end.

'F-father, F-father,' Kenny repeated over and over as he took the punches and was thrown by a "leg and a swing" into the pond. The four boys ran off. Both the brothers just sat in the pond, the rain beat down onto their faces, washing away the dirt almost cleansing their body, mind and soul. David looked at Kenny and for a moment in time, they connected in another way. They were close as siblings, but the bond that seems to develop at this time seemed stronger, tighter and unbreakable, almost it seemed. They communicated but without words, understood what each one was thinking and feeling. Again the silence surrounded them, perhaps for the very last time.

They helped each other out of the pond and it was almost as if they had been enlightened with the whole experience.

They dragged their feet through the mud and then onto the road but instead of walking into their street, they continued on. The rain belted down on them but they continued their journey onwards. They finally caught up with the four boys, who were sheltering under the old house with ruins, which was at the end of their street. The bricks were all up in piles and the windows were boarded up. This house lay desolate and the bullies often "hung out" here, it was their den. The brothers walked in through the broken down door, walked over the bricks that had been scattered in front. The four boys turned around, started to laugh loudly as they approached them. David clenched his fists then Kenny copied him. They rolled up their wet shirts and jacket, revealing their arms. They lifted their arms up and stood in a boxing stance, this time their shoulders were strong and their heads held high.

'What's this, a joke? Just like the two of you?' came the menacing voice. The two brothers stood silent for a minute and their eyes firmly on the target. They knew it was time for their fists to do the answering back.

They finally reached the front door; it was very late but there was no one waiting for them out of concern. They stood still for a moment outside; Kenny reached into his pocket and took out some very wet elastic bands.

'H-here,' he said and handed one to David and kept one for himself. David let the rain wash his long hair back; he gathered all his hair and tied the elastic band around them. Kenny did the same. They both gulped the rain down and quenched their thirst. It had washed away the blood of their faces and they both felt warmth inside. The dark clouds circled above but both the brothers could feel the sun. 'A-are you ready?' Kenny asked,

'Yes,' said David. They both put their hands on the doorknob to turn it. It was time for answering back. They twisted the knob and both of them entered their house. The door slammed hard behind them.

Arranged Marriage

As an easy-going British Asian, life was so grand and being the youngest of six, it was even better. My parents, who had emigrated from India in the early 1960s, had made a home for themselves here. I have two older brothers and three older sisters. When my father came over from India, he came alone. When he had worked and brought a house, my mother, two brothers and two sisters joined him here. My eldest brother is fifteen years older than me. I know, wow, but my parents had four children in India and I and my sister over here in England, which explains the age gap.

Both my parents were illiterate and the only jobs found were factory work. So growing up, we saw one parent at a time because they both worked shifts. My father worked at night and my mother during the day but sometimes both on the weekends. My parents were not strict. So, we had a modern upbringing, simply because my older brothers and sisters were educated. It was our brothers who turned up to our parent's evenings.

Growing up in the early 1970s was magical; I loved my early school years and have fond memories of the teachers who I look back on with great admiration. This was a time when people left their back doors open without fear; neighbours were actually your neighbours and looked out for each other. I remember we had white neighbours, and sometimes on the weekend my father would make a curry for them, which they enjoyed.

We played out all day only coming into the house for something to eat. The park was one of my favourite places, our brothers would take us there over the weekends. The summer holidays were the best; the gleaming sun made us feel all warm inside. The bell-bottoms and full-collar shirts were unisex and I had a burgundy piece which I never wanted to take off; yes, those were definitely the days.

I attended an all-girls secondary school in the 1980s, which was good. Well, my perception of it anyways. To make life a little sweet guess what we had right next door to us? An all-boy's school, but that is another story. It was very different from junior school as the teachers were very strict. Our headmistress was quite harsh but firm. Being it an all-girls school, I suppose she had to be. There were no major issues of bullying, as minor incidents did happen but then everyone would jump in to help the other.

I made good friends, we learnt, we laughed, we skived school to go to the park and talk to the boys and had not a care in the world. After leaving school, I continued on to further education at college. This was a different experience all together, very laid back and socializing in the pub on a Friday afternoon. I don't drink alcohol, but the orange juice was lovely.

When I turned twenty and had finished college, my parents sat me down and asked if I had a boyfriend. Unfortunately, I did not. So, they briefly mentioned arranged marriage. First, I thought nothing of it, but then the idea of an arranged marriage did not seem too bad; it was almost like a blind date. I knew if I did not like the guy, my parents would never force me into anything, nor my brothers and sisters.

I decided to give it a go and told my parents that I was ready. My parents were delighted. Phone calls were made and the matchmakers were informed. The idea of dressing up and meeting a guy who could potentially end up being my life partner seemed ludicrous but I was intrigued by it all and wanted to experience this. The matchmakers were quick and keen. So, before I knew it, there was a line of "husbands to be" waiting.

I was very excited and both my parents and one of my brothers accompanied me to see a boy at a mutual house. I wore a simple Asian suit. I did not want to go all glammed up. The matchmakers were very nice; they had tea and samosas ready as we got there. But we sat and waited, as the boy and his family were running a little late. I thought, *Wells, that's a good start.*

Finally, they arrived, and he came with his parents and sister. The men sat in one room and the women in another, as they usually do. I was introduced to the mother and daughter, who I made polite conversation with but to be truthful I was not impressed with his mother, she seemed like a battle-axe and looked at me with disapproval which left me feeling uncomfortable.

After everyone had tea, it was time for us to meet, the boy had already been settled in another room on his own and I was escorted by the matchmaker to see him. I went into the room and he was sitting on the sofa settee. The matchmaker introduced us and left the door slightly opened as she left. I remember, he wore a grey trousers and a shirt but as soon as I saw him, I could hear "no-no" running through my mind. I mean he was quite good looking but I think I was a little fussy. He waffled on about; to be honest I wasn't listening.

He was happy listening to me for the five minutes he did give me to speak but then continued on about himself. He said he would like to take it further, perhaps another meeting where we are alone no family. I just nodded and mentioning that I needed a little time, in the back of my mind I could still see his mother's face staring at me. Tell you the truth I wanted to get out of there the faster we got in.

Back home my mother was happy.

'He seemed like a nice boy and he has a job what did you think of him them?'

'No mum I wasn't that keen,' I said.

'Any particular reason why?' she asked.

'Mum there was no connection, mentally, physically and spiritually,' I replied.

'Oh,' she gasped and we left it at that.

It did not get any better, I got to a point where I had seen four boys and the novelty was wearing of. I think I was looking for someone who kind of thought out of the box. As you can imagine my mother was fed up of going with me and then I turning them down, she said it was not nice to keep saying no to someone's son but what could I do, I was not easily impressed. My father used to joke all the time about everything, he was a happy man and he enjoyed the odd drop of Teachers' whisky after a hard day at work.

We laughed all the while about what I saw in all four boys. I told my father there was no point marrying them, some did not drink so my father would not have a drinking partner, some had no sense of humour and this was very important others not much else about them. I left it for a while, all that 'arranged marriage larking', felt it was not my cup of tea, and kept a low profile. I had finished college and decided to take a year out.

However, another opportunity came knocking on our door one Saturday afternoon, it was one of my father's cousin's brother's son. He was very adamant in fixing me up but I told him what had happened before and I wasn't really sure.

'He is my best friend, I have known him since college days and really good lad and his family are wonderful,' he explained.

Well, that was it. I really had nothing to lose. There was no harm I suppose in seeing him. My mother was upset when the day arrived, she said she didn't want to come as I probably end up saying no. So my father and brother went with me. I remember I wore my favourite yellow Asian suit, no jewellery, no make-up, just simple. We got to the matchmakers house and had tea. The boy was already there in the front room but he came alone. I was ushered into the room but this time the door closed behind me. I turned and looked around and saw this young lad sitting on the settee. He was wearing black trousers, a white shirt and a black cardigan.

'Hello,' he said.

'Hello,' I replied.

I sat on the settee opposite him, and we started to talk. We actually had a good conversation, laughed bit at arrange marriages and talked about his best friend.

His name is Kamlish Lal and at that time he just started as a salesperson in Curry's Electrical Store. I liked the name as mine is Kulvinder and I thought it had a nice ring to it. We continued to talk and he spoke about his family, which by the sounds of things was huge. He told me that his father has two brothers, and as he was growing up, the three brothers lived together with their families in one house. It was only when they were in their teen years that the brothers got their own homes and moved out with their children.

Can you imagine, in one house seventeen children, eight adults including the grandparents, unbelievable? But there was something about the way he spoke about his family, with passion and respect. I actually got swept away in the conversation and wanted to hear more. Then there it came, he told me that it is only fair to be honest upfront, he explained that he had no intentions of leaving his parents or moving out. I was a little dumbstruck but I thought if I don't ask him now then I never will.

'Can you tell me why you don't want to move into your own place?' I asked

He replied, 'Because my parents are damn good people.'

Well, well, the arrogance, I thought. *What more could you ask for?* Having good in-laws was a big thing because some of the horror stories that I have heard about them were scary. I started to laugh, and I knew this was the man for me. It wasn't just his words that reeled me in, he was very handsome, and there was something about that moustache he had. There was a knock on the door; his friend popped his head around and asked if everything was okay. We told him we needed a little more time; he had a big smirk on his face.

'Carry on, take all the time you need,' he said.

I think at this point in my life I actually felt happy, comfortable and content all that from one conversation. We decided to go back to our families and discuss it with them and then take it from there.

The matchmakers did not get back to us until two weeks later with the news that the boy was happy and to take the next step forward, to meet his family. Oh no, I was in a faff, felt nervous and said what if they did not like me? Well, it might not matter, but then again, it would be nice to get on with them. The time and place was arranged back at the matchmaker's house, this time with our families. It was only when we had arrived there that I felt quite ill. I think it was because I knew this was it, once I had met his parents, it would be all finalized.

The women were in one room and the men again in another. My father and brothers went to meet my husband-to-be and I went in to see my soon-to-be mother-in-law. When the door opened, I was baffled because there were, to my surprise, five fairly large women, sitting on the sofa settee. I smiled, simply, because I thought, *Which one is the mother-in-law?* Then I remembered to what Kamlish was saying about his family, all living together and making decisions as one. So, they had all come to see me. Oh, how nice!

As I stood there, my mother politely went around saying 'Hello' to all of them.

I was asked by one of aunties in the room to touch their feet as I said hello to them.

What!! Touch their feet!!

I thought I would never touch anyone's feet, this is ridiculous. As I was still thinking about this, my husband-to-be came into the room. When I saw his face, it slightly roguish but handsome with it; I lost all sense of what I was doing. He smiled at me. That was it, the butterflies in my stomach started to do somersaults. Touch their feet. Well, it was okay. I would touch his father's feet as well, if asked. My, what a day. My mother-in-law-to-be had a kind face; she was small and chubby and the hour we saw them for was very pleasant.

She explained that they are a very traditional family and would appreciate if I followed their tradition and to be fair, all the aunties were the same, very loving and happy. I was asked to go into the front room to meet my father-in-law and his brothers. This very tall man stood up from the chair, smartly dressed and smiled. I placed my scarf on my head and approached him; before I spoke to him, I touched his feet. Well, I thought it might as well fulfil the role properly if I was going to do this. It was all new to me but, again, my family was not that traditional where this one was.

New beginnings and a new life. We went on to get married six months later after our engagement. I knew that a boy who has been raised in a family full of love and laughter and taught to respect his elders had a positive start. After twenty-six years of marriage and still going strong, I still live with my in-laws, husband and my two children. I think the learning curb for me has been adjusting to a different kind of life prior to the one that I was used to.

I have to admit, at this point, that my husband was right. My father-in-law who I have named "the godfather" simply because when he walks into a room, you can hear a pin drop. Everyone just stops talking. Sometimes, life teaches you harsh lessons and my in-laws have been a tower of strength; they are the most genuine, loving people I have the fortune to meet. My sons love their grandparents and respect them the same.

First Love

Many people have had different experiences in life associated with their first love. Some cannot forget theirs, for some, it holds wonderful memories and yet there are others who have had a bad experience and just want to forget it. But for Parineeta, (Preethi for short), it was a very special time in her life and this experience also shaped her thoughts for the future.

Having gone to an all-girls secondary school in the early eighties, it was a time of excitement, a time for growing up and a time for making new friends. School was good, albeit strict. There was also an all-boys school right next door. As an easy going British Asian, Preethi went with the flow. Everyone had their own opinions about everything, where certain topics came, mainly discussions and arguments. There was one topic, however, that everyone understood and that was the subject of love.

Everybody knew everyone's business, who was going out with who, how long they had been dating and of course, the big question, was it real love? Holding hands was a very big deal back then, it really was; snogging was the next level which was an even bigger deal, but the ultimate sin was "being felt up". Oh My God, being felt up, how bad! When some of the girls used to discuss the fact that they had been "felt up", everyone listened intensively. The majority were too embarrassed to listening but at the same time too intrigued not to. Personally, it did not bother Preethi that much; it was no big deal, who cared?

At the age of thirteen, Preethi started to wonder about falling in love. She questioned herself whether it would happen to her and if so, when? Boyfriend—that word was so deep for her yet she paid no attention to it because that was something she thought she would never have. The reason for this was because firstly, Preethi was not a "looker". She had a side parting which was forever shaped into her hair. Secondly, wait for it, she had two plaits.

There were a couple of lads with whom Preethi grew up; they were just familiar faces, always dossing around on the street. She had an awful habit of going into the front room and watching the world pass her by. She would often see these lads standing around on the corner, holding carrier bags, bringing them up to their noses and sniffing glue. Every weekend, it was the same routine. It dawned on her one day as she watched why were they doing this? Something had to be done about it, but what could she do?

Then Preethi had a great idea (so she thought), she would write an anonymous note, warning them to stop or it would be taken further. Her cousin was cautious,

'You sure you want to do this?'

But her niece thought it was a good idea.

'At least it might stop them standing on corners and sniffing that glue!'

Anyways, Preethi wrote the note and plucked up the courage. She sneaked around to their house and posted it. This was on a Saturday evening. She went into her house, feeling pleased with herself, not realising that there would be consequences. As Preethi lay in her bed that night, she felt she had done a good deed. They would be scared by the note, stop sniffing glue and be good boys. Well, that was her thinking, at the time, until the next day about four o'clock when the doorbell rang…

Her cousin answered it; she shouted, 'It's for you.'

Preethi thought nothing of it until she came downstairs. Two of the lads were standing outside her house. The tall guy started to talk; all she got was mumbles until he took the letter out of his pocket that she had written and placed it on the wall. Preethi started to pay attention. He said they knew it was one of them and wanted us to write on a piece of paper so they could match the writing to the letter. *Oh bloody hell! What had she done! Was it that obvious to them?*

The heat on her face was unbearable. She ran inside, fumbling for a pen, advising her cousin and niece to change their writing so it wouldn't match the letter. Preethi was so scared; she thought the tall guy would be able to smell the fear on her. She pretended to write in a windy fashion, where she then told him that they knew nothing of this so-called letter and if he did not move, her father would make him. He put the letter back into his pocket. As he started to walk off, he suddenly stopped, turned around and stared at Preethi and then winked at her. She quickly ran inside, slamming the door shut behind her. That night, she lay on her bed, and she kept seeing his face. She had a warm feeling inside but also felt confused as the fear of him turning up on her doorstep still left Preethi unsettled.

The next couple of weeks were different. Preethi, her cousin and niece started to say hello to the lads as they passed by on the street. Besides, they saw them every day as they all went to the boys' school, next door. Preethi's eldest brother owned a fruit and vegetable store, just a couple of houses from where the tall guy lived. One Saturday afternoon, Preethi and her niece left her brother's store to walk home. Preethi popped into the chip shop, which was two doors away and fancied a hot bag of chips. Preethi had on, nice blue leggings with a net blue *kameez* and a burgundy jacket on top, that was her favourite Asian suit, which she wore with small black heels.

She came out of the chip shop and could see them sitting on the wall outside his house. Her niece changed her mind,

'No way, I am not going past all of them,' she said.

She ran back into the shop. *Bloody great,* Preethi thought, she had to walk past them by herself. As she approached them, she could hear wolf whistles. Preethi dared not look at them as she trembled past quickly. She carried on walking, so hot and flustered, relieved when she had turned the corner. Preethi opened the bag of chips from the top, slightly tore one side and had a chip. *Very nice*, she thought.

All of a sudden, Preethi heard a voice calling her name. She turned around and it was the tall guy following her.

'What do you want?' she asked.

'I want to talk to you,' he replied.

'What do you want to talk about?' she said.

As she crossed the road, he followed her.

Oh no, what is he doing? she wondered.

The fear set in. Now Preethi started to worry at the thought of her dad coming around the corner, catching her talking to this guy. As she tried to walk on, he came up behind her. Preethi stopped and there was an alley to her right. His actions made her back up in there. What was she thinking? She walked backwards and the guy kept coming towards her.

Her mouth became dry all of a sudden; and she felt her heart was in her mouth, and you know when you are scared for some reason, you can feel your heart beating in your throat? Preethi felt this was one of those moments. Well, anyway, they went part way down this alley; Preethi was still clutching her chip bag and he kept coming towards her without saying a word. He just stared at her. Preethi stopped.

'What do you want to talk about?' she asked again.

He just looked at her. Preethi turned to one side so he could move, but she went straight into the right side of the alley wall. He turned towards her and came closer. Preethi felt her back against the wall; he came even closer. Now, she was worried what his intentions were.

All of a sudden, he stood in front of her and put both his hands on the wall with his arms out, Preethi being caught in the middle. At this point, she became very confused. She still did not see this coming. Before she had a chance to say anything, he leaned his face forward, right by hers and kissed her. As soon as those lips touched Preethi's, her temperature just shot up. She could not control her heart as it was beating so fast. She didn't even know where the sweat on her hands came from, but could feel it. That kiss, he rubbed his lips on hers and Preethi could feel his moustache hair on her top lip, then he put his tongue in her mouth. OMG!!

The sensation that shot through her at this point, she could not describe, but she got the taste of beer and cigarettes in her mouth. Her whole body was in a trance for a couple of seconds and her legs started to shake. As he moved away, Preethi was stunned.

'You're going out with me now, okay,' he said.

He walked backwards, staring at her all the time, he got to the front of the alley then he disappeared. The heat on her face was uncontrollable and was red raw as she came out of the alley. Her legs trembled; her heart was thumping like it was going to jump out her mouth. Preethi tried to walk home fast but her knees kept bloody knocking together. She was scared and wanted to get home before he came back.

When Preethi finally got home, she went straight upstairs and lay on her bed, still quivering at what had just happened. The flashbacks of his face, his long swaying hair, his moustache and his mouth were continual. Every single time she thought of his eyes staring at her, she had to shut hers. Preethi thought of what had just happened and felt embarrassed. How was she going to face him? They had school the next day; she was bound to see him. Hell! Her cousin was painting her nails in the front room and Preethi went down to tell her.

'That horrible lanky one?' she gasped.

'He's bloody ugly,' she said.

Preethi felt so hurt at that comment because of what had just happened. Actually he was not ugly, far from it, with his canvas jacket and Farah trousers, he was gorgeous and that kiss…

Preethi was smitten. Was it love? Was it the start of something special? Well, it felt like it to her. Preethi had got a boyfriend. Oh my God! She wasn't even asked out, but Preethi didn't mind as she was so happy. That evening, as the dust settled, Preethi lay on her bed staring at the ceiling. She kept seeing his face then remembering his actions. Each time she thought of him kissing her the way he did, the butterflies somersaulted in her stomach. Preethi finally nodded off towards the early hours of the morning because her thoughts were just buried in his face.

At school, one of his friends found Preethi and told her to wait for "her boyfriend" by the park gates in the afternoon. Preethi had never skived off school before; this was going to be the first time. That afternoon they met up and spent the rest of the day in the park, walking and talking and of course holding hands. The better part of the week was spent this way. On Saturday morning, her father was at work doing overtime, and her mother and aunty were getting ready to go to London. Preethi had relatives there, and her mother and aunty were going up for a visit. It was pissing it down…rain, rain and more bloody rain. Preethi could go nowhere or do nothing.

Her cousin was on the phone, as you do when your parents go out, get on the phone to everyone. The doorbell went about three o'clock. Preethi couldn't be bothered to get up, so her cousin answered it. She shouted at the top of her voice that it was for her. Preethi was comfortable, not wanting to move off her bed. Preethi came down, opened the door and saw her boyfriend on the other side of the street, leaning on the wall in the pouring rain.

'What?' Preethi shouted.

'Come out,' he said.

'No,' she replied.

'Just for five minutes, please,' he said.

'Okay, five minutes,' Preethi said, she felt bad that it was raining hard and he was just waiting for her.

Preethi found the umbrella and told her cousin she was going out. Her cousin just waved, as she was too busy on the phone. Preethi had her biscuit-brown colour velvet *shalwar* and *kameez* suit on and of course her favourite burgundy jacket. She walked to the corner of the street and there he was, wet as a rat. Preethi put the umbrella over him. He just grabbed her close to him. He looked down at her, into her eyes, his wet hair dripping onto her face. Preethi turned her face and put it on his chest. It was raining, and Preethi was burning up. He held her so tight, she could hear his heart beating. Preethi couldn't look into his eyes; she felt too many sensations and the feeling that she got when she did, she could have easily just melted into him.

He was soaked and soon so was Preethi. He put his wet hands on her face to turn it towards him. Her eyes were closed; Preethi dared not open them.

'No,' she said softly.

'Yes,' he replied and kissed her.

The umbrella just fell to the side, out of her hands. Have you ever been kissed? When the rain is beating down on you and the wind is blowing? The rain just caresses and cascades off your face. His hands gently touched her face and the rain had made her face feel silky and smooth. Preethi thought it was time to be adventurous, so she took the risk.

As he kissed her and pulled away, Preethi pulled him back and for the first time she put her tongue in his mouth. He stopped and pulled her back.

'Really,' he said.

Preethi just nodded. That was it; she saw his face came into hers and as he did, he closed his eyes and he kissed her. The more the rain came down, the more they kissed…oh what a fantastic feeling that was, what an experience! Preethi was in love; she loved him and there would never be anyone else. Preethi thought her boyfriend was the love of her life; those thoughts which were running in her mind as he held her hand and walked her home, that moment in her life, Preethi would cherish forever.

***

For the Love of Cricket

The glorious club came forward in all their suited and
booted attire
The trousers and t-shirts and sweaters was a sight for sore
eyes to admire
The teams waited and anticipated, with caps, gloves and
boxes intact
The ground was just perfect, ready for the match

For a moment the earth stood still as the coin was tossed into
the crisp air
It shone brightly in the sun as it came flickering down just
like waves making subtle flares
A solid decision was made, like the writing set in a stone
The men had scattered onto the ground, as if this is all they
have ever known

The two umpires are ready for action, with their eager eyes
on the game
No one can try and pull fast ones, for there will be nothing to
gain
The umpires hold all the cards and you will get what you are
dealt
For they have their secret weapon the third umpire, under
their belt
The bowler rotates his shoulders and gives his legs a shake,
Feeling comfortable and happy and ready to embrace,
This moment in history to start of the game as the umpire
hands over the ball
Which is hard and strong the stitches across the middle are
short not long

This ruby red is in the centre of it all, this beauty will be watched by everyone, big and small
This ball is a celebrity in its own right, as it's been hit, caught, dropped, lost, batted and bowled
The beamer misses the batsman but it's a close call, the umpire is not impressed, it's a "no ball"
The crowd is up on their feet shouting "no way", umpire is very strict, and how can they play

The verdict it is clear as can be, the bowler's foot was over the line,
The captain's delivery is a disappointment, before even starting, it is looking to decline
The game got off on the wrong foot but now it is in full swing
This is a delight to watch, for the fans are being entertained in this ring

There are boundaries flying all over this glorious precious pitch
Even at one point, it started to rain sixes without any hitch
Two-forty was the score when they were finally done
But now it's the turn of the fielders who stood under that hot sun
Time for a break, biscuits, lemonade and tea, everyone's watered, fed and refreshed
There is no suspending this game, as the weather is stupendous and there is no chance of rain
They are heading for a century, score just a little less; this second half is anybody's guess
As the partnership is formed, the pressure is now on, "six, six" up and away that is gone, gone

There are 20 balls remaining and they need 35, the tension is growing very high
There goes a stumping and "oh he's out", the batsman lets out a huge sigh

Last man comes out can he be the saviour, is this the moment of truth?
The fielder's threw the ball, it hit the wicket, but the batsman's on the floor, what a move!

All eyes fixed on the screen, is he out or is he in and he is out, what a game!
A spectacular finish they have all delivered well, they all belong in the hall of fame
The ending was crucial and that wicket keepers catch and his superb stumping
For the love of cricket has left the fans' hearts pumping

My Mother

My parents immigrated from India in the early 1960s and due to the fact that they were both illiterate, the only jobs they got were working in a factory. My mother did the day shift and my father did the night shift. As the youngest of six, my mother was in her early forties when I arrived. So over the years as I was growing up, many people believed that she was my grandmother due to her elderly appearance. Her hair was white with bits of grey like white snow with subtle greyish in and her eyes were smoky blue. I had often wondered growing up why she had blue eyes and the rest of us all had dark brown eyes. Her eye colour had changed over the years from dark brown to blue because of the environment she had worked in at the factory. Her cheeks were full of colour and warmth, which were soft to the touch. She had this long grey coat with lapels on the shoulders and it really was not that warm, it was quite light like a canvas material. Her headscarf was the best, the print on it was of horse's head and horseshoes, which was repeated all over. It was beautiful and made out of silk.

She was full of life; very independent; here, there and everywhere, she hardly stayed at home, and the buses were her best friend. She had this black woven basket which was like a spider's web and if you caught your fingers in-between, they were difficult to get out. Her famous umbrella she never left behind and took it with her wherever she went. What you saw was what you got. She had nothing to hide and her love was so warm and tender that we could not do without. She set the rules and maintained discipline in a strict manner. My father was a jovial man, always laughing about something even nothing. Now he was a push over so to speak. We could easily sway him to our way of thinking. My mother had acknowledged wisdom over the years, which she repeated to us on a regular basis, like, 'There is nothing you cannot accomplish if you try. You make your bed then you lie in it, and you are responsible for your own actions, sorry should be in your vocabulary.'

It was just before Christmas and she had complained about her leg, which was hurting her for a couple of days; I decided to take her to the hospital as she was in a lot of pain. As they assessed her, they decided to keep her in for observation. Well that was it.

'How long do I have to stay here?' she said.

'Not long, Mum. Once you are better, they will let you out,' I told her.

The two days turned into a week, by now all my family was in and out of hospital, taking turns to see what was going on. As I mentioned I am the youngest of six siblings, so all of us rotating around the hospital when we could. My two older brothers had spoken to the doctors and I could see that there was something more going on but was not sure to what it was. I went to see my mother. She was lying down on the bed, and she seemed frustrated.

'I feel much better. Ask them how long before I can go?' she asked.

'They are probably discharging you right now Mum, I do not think it will be any longer now,' I told her.

As my brothers came in and sat down, they spoke to my mum about any pain she might be having.

'No-no-no, I feel much better. Ask the doctor when I can leave,' she told them.

'They are keeping you over the weekend just to make sure everything is okay,' my older brother reassured her.

As we left the hospital, my older brother told us all that there was a "family meeting" at his tonight, emergency.

My older brother started to talk my sisters and I listened carefully. For a minute everything seemed to go blur and all I could see was my sister's hands on their faces, crying. I really could not hear anything at all. I saw my brother approach me like he was miming words but I could not hear them.

'Are you okay? Kulvinder, can you hear me?' he said as if I had come out of something.

'What did you say? I did not hear you and why is everyone upset?' I asked.

'Cancer…She has cancer…There is not much time left,' were his words.

I can honestly say that the floor did collapse beneath me. We all hurdled together, thinking of what had happened and going up to the hospital to tell her. My tears were like an ongoing tap at full speed, not stopping. We had to be brave to give her this bad news; we couldn't be seen crumbling or breaking, which in fact we were. It all went pear shape from here, as we all battled our own insecurities about what was to come. I could not bring myself to be in the room when she was told so I sat outside, waiting. It seemed like a very long time before my brothers and sisters came out then I went in. I always remember that smile she gave me as I walked in. I could not cope broke down hysterically, I know it was wrong but my emotions got the better of me.

'It is okay, I have lived my life and have no regrets,' she said. I could not believe what I was hearing, such acceptance how could this be? Knowing that you might not wake up the next day and what about the rest of us? Her arms were wrapped around me tight and the warmth just left me exhausted.

My mother coped in the best way she knew, smile on her face taking each day as it came. The rest of us were quite lost to where or what we were supposed to be doing. She stayed at the hospital for two months and then they told us to take her home for her last days so to speak. My brother had re-arranged one of the rooms downstairs to suit my mother's needs. She was very fragile at this point, bedridden and in a lot of pain. I was responsible for her medicine being the first aiders in the family. We took turns to sleep in the bed next to her in case she needed anything during the night. She came on the Monday and by Friday it was my turn to stop at my brothers to help and support. She stopped talking by now and could not cope with noises so we were very quiet around her. I had given her medicine and she seemed to go to sleep. I watched her face as the expressions changed; she seemed peaceful at first and then a look of pain and struggle and then nothing, just sleep. We all seem to be floating like balloons bopping up and down in mid-air, just lost. I sat in the chair wondering what it would be like without my mother in the world; all of a sudden she woke up.

'How are you feeling mum?' I asked,

'Aching, all over in a lot of pain, another tablet?' she asked.

I gave her more medicine; I felt awful knowing this was the only way. The colour in her cheeks had faded away and her skin felt taunt and cold. She was weak and it showed.

'Do you know how lucky I am? I know my time is near some people do not get the chance one minute they are here and the next they are gone,' she said.

Lucky is that how she saw it, she kept her strength mentally, there was no doubt about that and a couple of days earlier she was tying up loose ends with my brothers, perhaps that is what she meant. I had to leave the room to gather myself and my sister-in-law went to sit beside her. The women who never sat still for a moment, always up and about doing things was just lying there, trapped on that bed, waiting just waiting. On Sunday evening, it was very late about 11.00 pm and I was getting ready to go home, my mother seemed much better today. Talking and laughing with us all, reminiscing about old times, coping. I kissed my mother on her forehead and told her that I would see her tomorrow; she kissed me back softly on my cheek. I turned back and looked at her lying on the bed, she waved and I waved back.

It was about 2.00 pm the same night, when I got the phone call from my brother; my mother had passed on peacefully. I sat for a while, thinking how three hours earlier I was talking to her.

Passing of Time

The silence was like a smell of roses drifting in the air, all around the house,
This suddenly broke at the news of a new bounce,
Music filled your ears and the whole room with laughter and joy,
After the magic words were spoken, 'It's a boy, it's a boy!

The pitter-patter of tiny feet got stronger and stronger,
Before you knew it like an endless summer the days got longer and longer.
He always wants to keep his thumb in his mouth,
My instructions are clear I go north but he will still go south.

Bath times are fun like we never knew,
Just a big old tin bath we shared with a few,
Bedtime stories like a golden hour, pirate ships and adventures galore,
Where did all these books come from? He wants more and more.

Tantrums had you at a gunpoint making you say 'yes do', not don't,
School dinners and lunch boxes battled it out,
Dirty knees and dirty uniform, Oh,
Time for a cup of tea, what is all the fuss about?

Tears like waterfalls cascading down tables and walls,
Homework and television always having a fight,
Day in and day out which one is wrong and which one is right?

Exams and girlfriends came at once like a storm looming over
ready to pounce.

Son and fiancé move in together just like the perfect weather,
Successful jobs no need to worry,
'We are getting married', we don't need to hurry,
Venues, invites, crockery and food, you are almost at the end
of your tether.

Who is this with a beautiful face, like an angel full of grace,
Surely there could not be any other,
Time has passed by, like a fast pace,
Yes it is true, you're a grandmother.

The Last Leaf

The little boy stood at the bottom of the tree, staring up at this gigantic bark before him. It was an old tree you could tell from the size of it and the worn away bark on some of the places on the trunk. This once beautiful rich dark brown bark was now grey and dark with moss growing in between. Some of the bark had come away and the inner side of this tree was visible. Yet it was enormous and had a sense of proud about it. It branched out as far as it could, almost like you would branch out with your arms, hands and your fingers stretched as far as you can stretch them.

The little boy signed as if there was no activity here to engage him. He pondered backwards and forwards, almost to say, 'how boring'. The tree was still as it towered over the little boy. The little boy stood for a while looking and staring into space, he turned around to walk off and then suddenly he heard a sound. It was quite faint at first; he could not make out what it was. First quietly then slowly it got louder and louder, the wind was howling. The leaves stirred at the foot of the tree, almost coming off the ground but then fell back instantly. The tree was almost bare as most of the leaves had fallen down. The leaves had been stripped away from the branches to show their nakedness. The tree was once full of leaves and the colours were a "sight for sore eyes", as it could be spotted for miles. Now the twigs limped, drooped down and seem to hang in shame. But there was hope yet.

One remaining, brightly coloured orange and red leaf, desperately hung on. He had grown up on this tree, matured beautifully. He had felt the sun on his back and the rain gliding off him. His sisters and brothers had often looked down at the world beneath them. They had laughed so many times, whispered as people stood underneath them and took photos. They praised each other if a camera had got close enough to take an individual picture of the leaves. At night they had huddled together, relaxed and calm and in the day showed off their glory.

As this sad part of the year had returned, it was time to say goodbye, but this one leaf remained intact. He wanted to enjoy the moments from above, the scenery he had witnessed over time. He gathered his thoughts, reminiscing about the experience he had had. The stories that he could tell of the ordinary lives of people who walked past the tree, stood still to observe it and even those who had leaned on it to kiss.

But now there was a storm coming, it was as if he was fighting for his life to stay attached to the tree but the wind had a different idea. The colours of the leaf changed as it flapped about with the wind, the orange vividly caught your eyes and then the red they kept swapping with the change of the gust. The twig on the branch seemed strong to keep this connection held together as long as possible. This leaf was not giving up hope. This wind howled louder and gushed up the heap of leaves around the foot of the tree, bringing them up the whooshing them down again. The single leaf held on. Again the wind came back with a vengeance, the scurried up leaves buzzed, circling the bark and then scattering back down.

The wind was too strong. All of a sudden there was silence, no wind. The quietness filled the surroundings. Then, just like magic, the last leaf broke away from the branch and gently made its way down to his sisters and brothers, onto the ground. They lay there for a while just to savour the moment. The last leaf had joined the rest. The wind made the leaves dance again, like a whirlwind around the tree, to display of triumph of its success. The wind had managed to bring the last leaf down. Her work was done here and she moved onto another tree. After a while the leaves settled and then there was silence. The little boy, with his eyes and mouth wide open, shouted at the top of his voice, 'Wow,' as he stood still at the bottom of the tree, still looking up.

The Room

The sun was shining bright and its warmth graced Robert's face, he stood outside the house for a while, taking it all in. He began to approach the front door, the waiting game was over. Robert almost slammed the door behind him as he slid across the marble floor, nearly missing the banister he leapt up the stairs missing two steps at a time. His hands cascaded of the beautiful oak railings, all the way to the top. He gathered himself in front of the door, straightening his tie and running his fingers through his hair. Then he let himself in, his eyes prized over the room, the portraits on the wall seemed to talk to him, welcoming him in. On the desk before him where the letters sent to him from his father, some opened some still sealed, the ones his mother kept hidden from him. His fingers skimmed over the few books left on the bookshelf, some felt rough and roguish others smooth as silk.

His father was a busy man who had a huge amount of wealth, not just from his services to his country but also from the business he had founded from an early age. He felt distanced from his father whom he seldom seen and his mother had suffered over the years from loneliness and her abuse of alcohol. When she drank, it was a good idea not to be in the same room as her because quite often this meant a dark time for Robert. It was not just the verbal abuse but the near misses of physical abuse also. Robert despised his father for not being there for him, blaming him for his mother's state of mind and health but he was blinded by his love for his mother.

But now, Robert focused on the room he was standing in; the open fire was roaring inviting him closer to the leather chair with its back turned to him.

'At last,' Robert mumbled, 'At last.'

The chair swerved around and the figure sitting on it stood up.

'Oh Father, I have missed you so much,' he cried out.

Today was the day Robert did not care; he fell to his knees in front of his father, placing both his hands over his face. The few fond memories that he held of his father from his early years had been trampled on by his mother, leaving no room for love, just hatred. His tears rolled out onto his face, bringing out the hurt and pain that Robert had endured. He wanted to get rid of all the distress that his mind and body has suffered and this was the best way to washing it all away. His father's embrace lifted Robert from his knees, the weight on Robert's shoulders had disappeared and Robert felt himself rising up like a glorious star. They stood for a very long time just holding each other like there was no tomorrow. There was a knock on the door and Robert gently moved away from his father.

'Come in,' his father replied, wiping his eyes.

It was only Mrs Wetly, the old housemaid, who had devoted her entire life to the Gateleys, bringing in the afternoon tea. Her white bony fingers grasped the tray which shook with every step she took. Robert had a flashback; once how his mother had threw the "cheap wine" bottles over Mrs Wetly's head and demanded vodka and whiskey instead. Mrs Wetly slowly picking up the broken glass without a word and then glancing over to Robert, looking at him in despair. Robert opened the door for her; she had reached out one hand and stroked his face, in sympathy. There was another time when his mother complained about her to his father on the phone to let her go but his father had refused.

'That old cow needs to go, she cannot even get one job right,' his mother hissed.

Robert had comfortable warm feeling inside, he was happy and content. The bitterness that had been embedded in Robert by his mother had gone.

'I love you Robert my boy, always has,' his father said choking on his words.

'She was very sick, son, unstable mentally,' his father said shaking his head.

His mother had run up high debts ranging from clothes, antiques and dead end properties, things not necessarily needed but wanted. His father could not earn the money fast enough for it to be squandered on frivolous things. Not having the money to waste added pressure to his mother. She retaliated by using the only important thing she had, Robert.

The room had lit up creating a moment of magic; it was a far cry from the room he once grew up in. Robert never thought this day would come it was only by chance that it did. Only a few weeks ago he had stumbled upon the open safe his mother had left while being under the influence of alcohol. Robert was 9 years old when he last saw his father but now he was a man. As soon as he touched the letter, he knew something was not right. Some had been left open others not even looked at and some burnt at the edges. A deep pain developed in Robert's heart, he just knew. This time the flashbacks appeared quickly in his mind. The image of his mother ranting and raging that his father had neglected him, wanted nothing to do with him. Robert felt really sick in his stomach, knowing that this was not the case.

'But why, Oh why,' he kept repeating the same words.

His tears had ran then dried and then ran again, leaving his face feeling grubby, wet and cold. He seated himself against chair by the window and started to open and read some of the letters. His father had written to Robert four times a month telling him of his travels and the world that lay before him. His later letters turned in plea to his mother, begging her to see his son. Robert had had enough, it was time to ask questions to the only person who could answer them. He remembered that day, very well…

Refusing to eat dinner again, his mother was in her bedroom. Robert did not knock but entered unannounced.

'What is the meaning of this dear?' she spoke, softly.

Robert said nothing but placed some of the letters in front of her. She got up not realizing what they were then all of a sudden her expression on her face changed; she went almost as white as a ghost.

'Robert my love you must understand,' she pleaded.

'You had no right Mother, to do this this, no right at all,' Robert replied.

'Your father was never here, I had to take of everything and you, where was he? Where?' she snapped.

Robert had seen this before but it was too late as she swung around the half empty bottle of vodka was clearly visible in her hand. Robert needed to leave, quickly. He walked towards the door but she had grabbed him from behind. Robert was not a child anymore but a man; as much as he loved his mother he was not afraid anymore. He looked at his mother, almost feeling sorry for her but then now the truth had surfaced and it needed to be dealt with.

'Did you ever stop to think, did you? About me growing up without a father's presence? I could understand for those whose fathers have passed away. But mine was alive but you destroyed any chances of me being with him. All those years I hated him but for what and all those lies you had told me, all lies, lies, lies!' Robert felt distraught to a point where he just wanted to burst crying.

'Grow up, would you? That's all I have got—a useless husband and a sniffling little boy!' she snarled.

Robert turned away. He was done. He moved towards the door slowly. He felt a sharp pain in his head; he realized quickly that his mother had grabbed his hair on top of his head. Robert could feel the pain running over his scalp.

'Mother, stop!' he cried out in pain.

He held her hand and prized it away from his head. She stood swaying from side to side, drunk.

He got to the door and turned around.

'Goodbye Mother,' were his last words to her.

He could hear her shouting as he left the house but soon the screams died down. It was shortly after this that Robert's grandmother had come and took his mother under her wing to her house, out in the country. Robert had got in touch with his father who by now had lost all hopes of seeing his son. The room where he was held hostage, for years by his mother, was now a sanctuary, for this is the same room where he met his father for the first time in years.

The Room

Characters:

Pamela Gateley: A 57-year-old mother and of leisure, also an alcoholic

Sarah Tunstall: Pamela's mother, 77 years old and a wise lady

Mrs Wetly: The 70 years old housemaid

Gabriel Hynes: A gentleman caller, 50 years old

Scene 1: In the Room on a Rainy Afternoon

Pamela and Gabriel walk in DSL, take their coats off and start to talk while entering the room.

Pamela:	Really, Gabriel. Is this necessary? How much is it this time?
Gabriel:	Oh come now, Pamela. It is an investment for your future…for Robert.
Pamela:	I really think it is not possible this time; there is too much at stake, but you know this already.
Gabriel:	(*Starts to make a drink for PAMELA at US*) You really are beautiful when you are being defiant, that is what I like about you, always have. How about I take you to the theatre next week just the two of us and make a night of it, perhaps dinner afterwards?
Pamela:	Theatre? (*PAMELA sits down on the sofa*) That would be lovely; it has been a while since I have been.

Gabriel walks towards her and puts the drink on the table. Puts his hands out in front and Pamela holds them and stands up. He holds her in his arms, whispering in her ear.

Gabriel:	I will return the money; I have just come up short. Have I ever let you down? It's not that much, just 15000, Pamela. That really is just pocket change to you. You know I have a couple of investments but at the moment it is just difficult to get hold of the funds. I will be

	sorted in two weeks' time then I will come and see you and return your money.
Pamela:	(*Breaks away from his embrace*) Oh, Gabriel. You are a devilish man. What am I to do with you?
Gabriel:	Pamela, all these years, who has looked after you? Given you the love and attention that you deserve. If only you had listened to me and divorced that man, we could have been living a good life. It is not enough just sending a cheque to you every month. He is still sending you the money, isn't he? I mean of course he is. He has a son to look after. Well, I have to say Pamela, he is a generous man, indeed.
Pamela:	(*Walking towards DSL, looking out into the audience and then towards GABRIEL and frowns*) It is not just about the money, Gabriel. I have been left alone all these years without any companionship, except Robert.
Gabriel:	What about me Pamela? Don't I count for anything? (*Pamela walks towards DS and turns around looking at Gabriel*)
Pamela:	What about the others Gabriel? I cannot compete anymore; there is always someone else. Why just the other day Murial, you remember her? I met her at the County Club. She said she saw you with Belinda and the two of you seemed very close? Belinda was laughing and I believe you were holding her quite close?
Gabriel:	(*Comes up behind PAMELA and speaks angrily towards her*) Who? Murial, Belinda? Pamela there is no one else and really you should not be delving in gossip. They have nothing to do in their spare time but talk about good people. I was

	simply comforting her, little Lousia had fallen in the garden and broken her arm. What was her name again? I forget, Belina, Belinda not sure but I have seen her around, I thought it was just polite to ask after the little girl. You know Pamela my nature like to help others as much as I can.
Pamela:	Have I really got nothing to worry about? (*Pamela goes and sits back onto the sofa, picking up her drink*) In that case I will have this drink and another, that's that then.

Mrs Wetly knocks on the door DSL, walks in without being told to. She stands and stares at Gabriel with disapproval.

Pamela:	Yes?
Mrs Wetly:	Mrs Tunstall is here, your mother.
Pamela :	(*PAMELA gets up almost in a panic, tries to put her glass on the table, turns to GABRIEL with a look of concern*)
Gabriel:	You really need to put your foot down Pamela, I know your mother does not like me but after all these years she must of mellowed? Or is she still devoted to her son in law? Why she doesn't warm to me I don't understand, can't she see how good care I take of her daughter?
Pamela:	Gabriel, please you do go on, you need to leave right now. It must be important. Mother never comes at a drop of a hat, she calls first.

Mrs Wetly leaves the room DSL, looks around one more time at Gabriel with a side smile as if to say, time for you to leave. Pamela quickly pours another drink and knocks it back.

Pamela:	Gabriel, I will have the money for you tomorrow but you need to go now.
Gabriel:	No Pamela, I will greet your mother first.

Pamela: I do not want any arguments right now, it is best if you go, you now it will turn ugly.

Mrs Wetly walks in again without knocking this time, she seems disappointed but stands by the door.

Mrs Wetly: I am afraid Mrs Tunstall has gone, when I returned downstairs and looked around she had left, I believe she might have seen Mr Hynes's car parked at the back.

Pamela: That will be all Mrs Wetly, thank you.

Mrs Wetly leaves DSL, slightly slamming the door on her way out.

Pamela: (*Pours another drink and sits comfortably on the sofa, letting out a sigh*) So glad Mother's gone but I wonder what she wanted?

Gabriel: (*Sits next to PAMELA and puts his arm on the back of the sofa, smiles at PAMELA*) Forget about her Pamela, you think too much, does it really matter. You know you should think about the important things in life. Finish your drink, I will pour you another. You know I care about you a lot, tell you what I shall take you shopping tomorrow, yes? I will be here first thing in the morning just to sort out my little financial matter. (*Gabriel raises his voice*) Once that little business is out the way, we will go out and buy a new dress for you?

Pamela: Yes. (*Leans over and rest her head on GABRIEL shoulder*)You are so good to me Gabriel; I really don't know what I would have done without you

Gabriel: (*Snuggles up to PAMELA*)
             You are right Pamela, the things I do for you, the things I do for you.

End of scene one, curtains close.

Scene 2: In the Room. In the Evening.

The room beautifully furnished with antique furniture and soft carpet. Mrs Wetly stands by the bar, fixing a drink for Pamela. Pamela sits on her comfortable sofa, finishing her drink. Sarah waits patiently, pacing slowly up and down the room for Mrs Wetly to leave

Sarah: How long, Mrs Wetly? (SARAH walks towards her, slowly) Never mind about that drink.

Mrs Wetly: (*looking around*) Nearly done dear, nearly done.

Pamela: (*Slightly drunk from drinking all afternoon but thinking she is okay*) Mother do sit down, you are making me dizzy all that walking.

Sarah: Pamela dear, I don't think that my pacing is making you dizzy.

Sarah walks and stands behind the sofa, CS, where Pamela is sitting facing forward. Mrs Wetly passes her the glass and slowly exits, SL. Pamela gets up from the sofa approaching the audience CS.

Pamela: (*Lifts glass up and out towards the audience before drinking, turns around slowly towards SR*) How about you pour yourself a drink, Mother? What is it, whatever is the matter?

Sarah: (*Sarah speaks quite harshly, looking straight at PAMELA*) More money was it? How much this time? I cannot bear to see his smug face, Pamela dear can you not see what that awful man is doing to you? He has been bleeding you dry from day one. It is not even his money my son-in-law has done more than enough to keep you comfortable in life. Yet you have squandered it all on a useless, good for nothing rogue.

Pamela: Come on Mother, what is wrong with you

Sarah: There are more important issues than Mr Hynes, and Pamela you need to listen to me

Pamela: (*Starting to speak with a slur, tries to put her glass down on the table*) What is it this time? I have been lonely Mother! Can you understand that?

Sarah: I don't even know whether you can hear me or not, just look at the state of you, Mr Hynes and your drinking. Lonely? Really Pamela and what about Robert? He has grown up into a wonderful man despite not knowing.

Pamela: (*Pretends to be listening*) Robert? He has had a very good life that I have given him! I provided for him. Yes Mother, I have taken good care of him. Robert didn't want for anything.

Sarah: (*Agitated and getting annoyed*) You looked after him? For what I have seen and know I think it is the other way around. How could you do this to him? How all these years he has believed everything you have said.

Pamela: I am not sure what you are trying to say. (*PAMELA walks towards the bar and fixes another drink*)

Sarah: Pamela, are you listening? (*SARAH biting her nails and looks around at PAMELA*) Pamela!

Pamela: Yes Mother? (*PAMELA comes from the bar and sits next to SARAH on the sofa*)

Sarah: (*Pauses*)

It is a question of time before Robert finds out the truth; I really do feel uncomfortable with this business, it is time he knew about his father.

Pamela: (*Gets up and goes towards the corner bar and retrieves a half bottle of vodka*) Really Mother it is too late; it wouldn't make any difference now. Let Robert think what he does, it is better for him what he does not know won't hurt him.

Sarah: (*Sarah raises her voice*) He needs to know, and if you don't tell him, I will. I cannot be a part of this anymore. I am guilty as you are. Why I let you talk me into this all them years ago and how…I really cannot remember. But now is time to do the right thing by Robert.

Pamela: (*Comes and sits on the sofa and looks directly at SARAH, starts to shout*) You will do nothing of the sort, Mother! That man, he was never here; I was left on my own with Robert, to suffer. I was alone; I had no one, and that man was off half way across the world.

Sarah: (*Sounding very concerned, gets up and moves away from PAMELA, SL*) Pamela, really stop. You let Robert think that his father did not care about him, neglected him, and wanted nothing to do with him! Oh my poor grandson, how he has suffered the times he has cried on my shoulder. I simply cannot do this no more can't you understand for once, Pamela. Stop being selfish. You are an alcoholic Pamela which has not helped you or Robert.

Pamela: (*Very upset and drunk, starts to cry*) You do know what this will do to me, Robert would end up hating me and for what? Do you really want this for me? I am your daughter,

	Mother. How can you think that after all this time I should let the truth out. Robert is my only child; I have kept him close and did this for his own protection.
Sarah:	(*Goes and stands by the desk at the window, looks out of the window and carries on talking to PAMELA*) You know, Pamela, I have doubts to how you have raised my grandson. Do you know what I mean? All those times, the look on his face when he was a child almost as if he was scared. You did that to him and I stood by and did nothing, nothing at all. This still haunts me.
Pamela:	I did nothing of the sort, why he was a happy boy. (*Slumps into the corner armchair by the built in bar and stops crying*) A little discipline never hurts no one and that's what I was simply doing, disciplining him since there was no father in his life. I had to do it all.
Sarah:	Yes, he was a happy child but you didn't see what I did. You were too drunk to notice.
Pamela:	(*Places the empty vodka bottle on the floor*) He was clothed, fed and content. What more does a child want?
Sarah:	(*Turns around from the window and goes towards DSL*) The love that he missed from his father, and a mother's love. You have made it even harder for Robert. When he realizes what is going on, I can't even think what he will go through. Pamela, you have made the wrong choices in life and as your mother I have stood by and let you, hoping that you will wake up and learn from your mistakes. But what you have done to Robert is unforgivable.

Sarah is clearly upset she sits in the chair by the desk puts her hands on her face for a while. She looks up at Pamela. Pamela seems in deep thought, staring into blank space. The patter of rain can be heard all around. There is silence for a while.

Scene 3:

Pamela is still awake; Sarah sleeps on the sofa, sitting up. Pamela puts down the cup of coffee and is at the point of sobering up. It 8.00 AM in the morning. The rain has stopped.

Pamela:	(*Speaks softly to SARAH*) Mother, Mother, are you awake?
Sarah:	(*Opens her eyes slowly, looking up at Pamela*)
Pamela:	I will get Mrs Wetly to make you some nice hot tea. (*PAMELA presses the buzzer on the table*)

Mrs Wetly has already prepared the tea and knocks on the door DSL.

Pamela:	Come in.
Mrs Wetly:	Good morning, Mrs Tunstall. How are we this morning?
Sarah:	(*Wide awake at this point and looks up at MRS WETLY*) Good morning, I have had better days, Pertuna.
Pamela:	That will be all, thank you.
Sarah:	(*Starts to drink her tea*) Pamela, please think about what I have said, it is in the best interest for Robert.
Pamela:	I will give it some thought Mother but I really do think that it is a waste of time.
Sarah:	(*SARAH gets up and puts on her coat and walks towards DSL*)
Pamela:	Will speak to you soon, Mother. Goodbye.
Sarah:	(*Looks back at PAMELA*)

	I hope next time we meet, Robert is here. Goodbye.
	(*SARAH Exits DSL*)
Pamela:	(*Gets up and walks to the desk, looks at the photo of Robert on the wall. Removes the photo revealing a safe on the wall, PAMELA searches frantically for the keys all over the room. Buzzes MRS WETLY. PAMELA sits at the desk waiting. MRS WETLY comes into the room DSL*)
Pamela:	What took you so long? I just need the keys, I have misplaced mine. I don't know why that husband of mine would trust you of all people. Give me the keys quickly! You can't even do any job properly. You really should retire now, somewhere, perhaps, way out in the country.
Mrs Wetly:	(*Looks at PAMELA, with a smile*) Here you go, the keys to the safe. I will stay as long as Mr Gateley wishes me to.
Pamela:	Mr Gateley, when has he ever been here? I've had to put up with you all these years not him. You can stay for a while; I will be finished soon, and I will give you the keys back, just hold on. (*PAMELA opens the safe and takes out a bunch of letter, sits at the desk and stares at MRS WETLY. MRS WETLY goes and sits on the sofa CS*)
Pamela:	What am I to do with these? (*PAMELA opens up some of the letters and starts to read one. She leaves the rest on the table, the one in her hand she throws into the open fire*)
Mrs Wetly:	What are you doing? No don't do that. (*MRS WETLY quickly grabs the poker and retrieves the half burnt letter*)
Pamela:	This is the only evidence. I must get rid of it. Robert must never know. I know what I need to do. I am going out for a while, put all these

letters back and lock up the safe. Keep the keys on you until I come back. (*PAMELA puts her coat on and dashes out the door DSL, MRS WETLY stays seated on the sofa for a bit. She slowly gets up and places the corner burnt letter on the table with the rest. She looks at the safe where all the other letters are, she smiles to herself, picks up the keys and puts them into her pocket. She picks up the tea-tray and slowly walks out of the room DSL, without closing the safe and leaving the letters as they were, on the table*)

The clock strikes, the time is three o'clock in the afternoon and ROBERT enters the room DSL, turns to MRS WETLY, asks her about his mother's whereabouts.

Mrs Wetly: No dear, I'm not sure where she is gone, but you are welcome to wait. I am sure she will be back soon. How about a nice cup of tea? (*ROBERT sits down on the sofa CS, he looks around the room and sees the safe open. He gets up and walks towards the desk SR*)

Curtains close.

Kulvinder Kherteru
Saturday, 25 March 2017
The Successor

This radio play is about a family who run business, where the Boss is looking to retire. He has two potential candidates to fill his position, his son and his PA. Both are experienced in different fields, but who will he choose? The setting is both in the office meeting room and the rest in their family home. The wife and the daughter add to the conflicts and change the dynamics of the play.

The Boss – John Jenkins, in his mid-sixties, very intelligent and experienced in his field.
The Wife – Marisa Jenkins, in her late-fifties, supports her husband in work and home life.
The Son – Marcus Jenkins, 30-year-old and is very ambitious and passionate about his work.
The Daughter – Lucy Jenkins, 28-year-old, her father's favourite child.
The PA – Bradley Harris, in his late-twenties, thrives to succeed in the company.

FADE IN ON NARRATOR. CALM MUSIC PLAYS IN THE BACKGROUND.

Scene 1

FADE IN ON OFFICE. WHIRRING SOUND.

At the office, the boss, the pa and the son.

THE BOSS: We need to finalise this deal. Once we are done, we can decide what to do next.

THE PA: Everything is in order. Now sir, about this presentation, do you want me to deliver it or Junior Jenkins? I really don't mind.

THE BOSS: I think you can take this one, Bradley, since you created it.

THE PA: As you wish Mr Jenkins. (FADE IN ON KNOCK. RATTLE OF CROCKERY) Ah, the trolley, thank you Mrs Brue. Sir, would you like a cup of tea?

THE BOSS: Yes I could do with one. (SOUND OF WATER POURING INTO A CUP) Where is Marcus? I haven't seen him yet? (SIGHS HEAVILY)

THE PA: I am sure there's a good reason for him being late; he was up until the early hours. Not sure but I think he might have been in the office bar having a drink.

THE BOSS: Was he? In that case, we had better start without him. We don't want to let the committee down. If we can convince the committee, on this one, then we are ready to go. There's a lot of work involved and I am glad, Bradley, that someone is prepared. If he

	was in the bar, he might be a little worse for wear this morning. (LAUGHS OUT LOUD)
THE PA:	You're right, sir. It might be a good idea to let him sleep it off. (CLEARING HISTHROAT) I like to be one step ahead, knowing where we are at and where we are going. Once this is over, we can think about the final details of our proposals. There should be no problems at all. I think that the committee will be bowled over.
THE BOSS:	You're very confident all of the time; that's what I like about you, my boy! I have to say you haven't let me down yet.
THE PA:	And I don't intend to Mr Jenkins, just doing my job.
THE BOSS:	Well you do more than your job; it's time, shall we?
THE PA:	Ready as always, I will go and check if all the committee are ready to come in.
THE BOSS:	That's a good idea; I'll just make a quick phone call to see where Marcus is.
THE PA:	That's fine, sir. You carry on.

FADE UP ON DOOR OPENING. HEAVY BREATHING. PAPERS SPILLING ONTO THE TABLE.

THE BOSS:	Marcus, what happened? Where have you been? We were just about to call them in.
THE SON:	Morning, Father. How are you? Oh damn, this briefcase. You ready to start?
THE BOSS:	It is nice of you to join us. Yes we are. Bradley's got everything under control.
THE SON:	Ah, reliable old Bradley! Are you sure you have everything?
THE PA:	Yes of course, Junior. I double-checked this morning.

THE SON: (IN A SARCASTIC TONE) Marcus is my name, not Junior. I have mentioned this before.

THE BOSS: (SIGHS GENTLY) Let's not start all this again, Marcus. It's only a bit of fun.

THE SON: No Father, you can call me that, but not Bradley. (PAUSE) He should know better.

THE PA: I was just teasing you Marcus; bit of fun that's all.

THE SON: Well, you've had your little laugh Bradley. Shall we, Father?

THE BOSS: Now boys, calm down. We have a lot to do this morning, let's go.

FADE UP ON MUTED TALKING AND LAUGHING. THE SOUND OF CUPS AND SAUCERS. THE SOUNDS FADE SLIGHTLY.

THE SON: So…How did you manage that, Bradley? What with all your experience, how could you have overlooked such an important point? I ask you Father, really, golden boy here, nearly cost us this whole quotation. Ah, yes he was prepared and the presentation was okay…not too bad, but the listings? Did you forget Bradley?

THE BOSS: (SIGHS WITH RELIEF) Well done, Marcus! Without the listings, we would have been very embarrassed. You got them here on time and this meeting was fantastic!

THE SON: You see, I went over the presentation last night and something was missing. I have been working until the early hours of this morning to do the listings. That is why I'm late.

THE PA: Well, thank you, Marcus, but I didn't forget. I thought we really didn't need them because the presentation carried itself, but perhaps, as

	Mr Jenkins has pointed out, it's good we had them as back up.
THE SON:	You know something Bradley, sometimes it is nice just to ask whether anything else might be needed. I asked you for the presentation, to look over, several days ago but didn't receive it until last night.
THE PA:	Marcus, the presentation has been lying on my desk. You could have easily picked up a copy, but it doesn't matter, the meeting was a success.
THE BOSS:	(LOWERING HIS TONE) Listen you two, this is not the time. (PAUSE) We need to see the committee members out. I am sure we can discuss this later
THE PA:	(QUICKLY REPLIES) Of course Mr Jenkins, I was just thinking the same thing. Marcus, let's just leave it now.
THE SON:	(RAISING HIS VOICE) Gentlemen please, I think we are all satisfied with the outcome. If you would like to make your way out, into the outer office, that would be much appreciated and thank you all for coming. It has been a pleasure.
THE BOSS:	(HAPPY VOICE) It has been a good morning, thank you all.
THE SON:	(SERIOUS VOICE) We will be in touch once the proposals have gone through.
THE PA:	(HAPPY VOICE) We appreciate your input. Thank you for coming, goodbye.

FADE UP ON DOOR SHUTTING. CHAIR PULLED FORWARD.

| THE BOSS: | (VERY HAPPY VOICE) Well done boys, that was great! |
| THE SON: | (SIGHS HEAVILY) I am really tired, Father...with all that work I did this morning. |

THE BOSS:	(LAUGHING LOUDLY) Are you sure, Marcus, it's not the one too many drinks in the bar last night?
THE SON:	Father, I told Bradley I was going home and to fax me the presentation. Did he not mention this?
THE PA:	(COUGHS) My mistake, Mr Jenkins. I thought Marcus returned to the bar.
THE SON:	(SOUNDS CONCERNED) This is really too much Bradley; seriously…you could have cost us!
THE PA:	Pardon, I don't think so, the presentation was bang on Mr Jenkins.
THE SON:	Yes, due to my listings, really Bradley, I think you should communicate with the rest of us before making any decisions by yourself. (PAUSE) Don't you think?
THE PA:	I think you'll find everything was in order Marcus, besides we got their business didn't we? You're really making a fuss over nothing.
THE SON:	That's not the point, Father, are you hearing this?
THE PA:	I think Mr Jenkins needs a break, perhaps a spot of lunch somewhere?
THE SON:	(ANGRY VOICE) I think I know what's best for my father, Bradley.
THE PA:	Why don't you join us Marcus?
THE SON:	Father, how can you just sit there and listen to this? Bradley, you really are out of order.
THE PA:	If you don't want to join us for lunch, (PAUSE) that is fine.
THE SON:	It's not about lunch Bradley; it's about you and how you conduct things around here.
THE PA:	Marcus, (PAUSE) I think you're tired. Maybe you need to go home and have a rest.
THE SON:	(RAISES VOICE) Don't tell me what to do. (HANDS SLAMMED ON TABLE)

THE PA:	It's merely a suggestion; you seem agitated.
THE SON:	Yes I am, thanks to you.
THE PA:	Well, if there is anything you need me to do, just say.
THE SON:	(IN A SARCASTIC TONE) Yes, there is Bradley; I would like you to shut the hell up.
THE BOSS:	(USES FIRM TONE) Look, we've had a good morning. Leave it at that.
THE SON:	(SOFTER TONE) Father, Mother's rang. Lucy's at home today.
THE BOSS:	We'll grab a bite to eat on the way. Marcus, let's go home.
THE SON:	I just want to wrap a few things up here Father, and then I'll meet you there.
THE BOSS:	In that case, I'll see you at home.
THE PA:	Mr Jenkins, if you want I can drop you of at the house? (PAUSE) I am going that way.
THE BOSS:	Jessop's already here.
THE SON:	Tell you what Bradley, I'll take Jessop. I've got one or two things to do so you can take Father home.
THE PA:	That's fine Marcus, will do that. Mr Jenkins, are you ready to go?
THE BOSS:	I don't like to keep Lucy waiting; my girl's at home, haven't seen her for a long time. (PAUSE) She seems awfully busy these days.
THE PA:	She's probably got a lot on after studying all those years, taking time out and now working. Plus, having her own place she's bound to be busy.
THE BOSS:	She hardly comes over any more. Always busy with her own things.
THE SON:	You know Lou, she will come over when she has time.
THE PA:	Yes that's true.
THE SON:	Yes thank you, Bradley, (PAUSE) Father's waiting.

THE BOSS:	Come on! Bradley let's go.
THE SON:	Father, tell Lucy not to go. I'll be there shortly.
THE BOSS:	Of course son, I will.
THE SON:	Don't know these days, her times so valuable. (PAUSE) I wonder if she's writing a book…
THE PA:	Mr Jenkins, (PAUSE) there's a flower stall on the way. We could get her some flowers?
THE BOSS:	That's a wonderful idea; yes of course, let's go. See you later son.
THE SON:	See you later, Father.

FADE

Scene 2

**FADE IN ON CLASSICAL MUSIC IN THE
BACKGROUND. SOUND OF CROCKERY BEING
PUT AWAY.**

*The father, the wife, the daughter and son at their home, just
finished having lunch.*

THE BOSS:	(V.O.) It was fantastic! (PAUSE) My boy's handled everything very well.
THE DAUGHTER:	Wish I was there to see that moment.
THE BOSS:	Bradley thought that we didn't need the listings? Perhaps, he had something else up his sleeve, but then Marcus had them as back up.
THE DAUGHTER:	(SIGHS HEAVILY) Oh Father, he's very good; he knows what he is doing.
THE BOSS:	You know Lucy, (PAUSE) he does and I am very proud of him.
THE DAUGHTER:	He works so hard all the time.
THE BOSS:	Yes we did. You are very concerned about your brother, Lucy?
THE DAUGHTER:	(PAUSE) Brother?
THE BOSS:	Yes, it's nice to see this bond between you both.
THE DAUGHTER:	(FIRM VOICE) Father, I'm not talking about Marcus.
THE BOSS:	You're not? (PAUSE) Oh are you concerned about Bradley?

THE DAUGHTER:	There is something I need to tell you, it might as well be now.
THE BOSS:	What is it Lucy? Is something wrong?
THE DAUGHTER:	No Father, what I was going to say is that I have some good news. I don't know how Marcus will react, but we will have to see. It's nothing to worry about, and I think you are both going to be very happy

HOLD VOICES, OVERPOWERED BY FEMALE VOICE SINGING 'OH WHAT A BEAUTIFUL MORNING, OH WHAT A BEAUTIFUL DAY.'

THE WIFE:	Lucy are you okay? (PAUSE) Marcus is just parking up, he's here.
THE DAUGHTER:	(CONCERNED TONE) I just wanted to speak to you both about something important, but now that Marcus is here, perhaps it can wait…
THE WIFE:	You sure Lucy?
THE BOSS:	Don't worry, it's only Marcus…
THE DAUGHTER:	(SIGHS) It's fine, I will talk to you both another time.

FADE UP ON DOOR CLOSING, SOUNDS OF KEYS THROWN INTO A PLATE.

THE SON:	Hello Lucy. (PAUSE) How are you? Good to see you…
THE BOSS:	Well done my boy, well done! (LOUD PATS ON THE BACK)
THE WIFE:	That was great Marcus, well done!
THE DAUGHTER:	Nice to see you Marcus, have you been busy? Working hard as I have heard from Father – Bradley did

	handle the presentation well, his hard work paid off too.
THE SON:	(SARCASTIC TONE) Bradley? Oh really, tell me Lucy what makes you think it was his hard work? Father, I think you need to enlighten Lucy on a few things.
THE WIFE:	Marcus, I know you have had a good day, but Lucy has some good news.
THE SON:	Okay sorry Mother…but I am intrigued to why Lucy would think this.
THE DAUGHTER:	No Marcus, I was just saying that's all. I am sure you worked hard also.
THE SON:	(ANGRY VOICE) Also?
THE BOSS:	Marcus, calm down, what's wrong with you?
THE SON:	Lucy thinks that I'm not pulling my weight…
THE WIFE:	Marcus, that is enough. There is no need to talk to your sister like that.
THE DAUGHTER:	I was just saying that I am sure you put in the hard work also. Come on, lighten up!
THE SON:	Okay Lucy, perhaps it has been a long night for me and a hectic morning. I'm sorry, Lou, it's nice to see you after a long time.
THE DAUGHTER:	Come and have some lunch, we've just finished. We got what we wanted, didn't we?

FADE IN ON OVAN DOOR OPENING. SOUND OF CROCKERY.

THE BOSS:	Marcus, you and Lucy are everything to me and your mother and we don't like the bickering.

70

	Marcus you should know better, Lucy is younger than you.
THE SON:	Sorry Father, I wasn't thinking – home-made pie, that's lovely, Mother. Lucy, how come you're so busy?
THE WIFE:	I thought I'd cook today as Lucy was coming over…
THE DAUGHTER:	Thank you Mother, that was really nice.
THE WIFE:	Since you came after a long time, you're welcome sweetheart.
THE BOSS:	Everything I have done in my life is for both of you and I'm not getting any younger, which brings me to my next point. Have I mentioned to you about me retiring soon?
THE SON:	Yes you have Father. You told me and Lucy three months ago.
THE DAUGHTER:	You have worked your entire life Father. It would be nice for you to spend time with Mother.
THE WIFE:	(GIGGLING) It would be great to have your father all to myself.
THE BOSS:	Well, (PAUSE) I have set certain things in motion, but will need someone to run the company for me. I mean, not just run it, but everything that goes with it to keep it as successful as we have done. There is a lot to think about and I know that both of you have worked your hinds off for this company.
THE SON:	(SIPPING WATER) Both of us?
THE BOSS:	Bradley and yourself, Marcus.
THE SON:	(SHOCKED VOICE) You're not serious Father?

THE DAUGHTER:	You are right Father; Bradley has worked alongside you for ages…
THE SON:	Lucy, am I missing something? I mean what I have achieved doesn't count?
THE DAUGHTER:	Marcus, you are getting too serious. We all know what you have done but you need to recognise Bradley's efforts also.
THE SON:	Why should I! Mr golden boy, how could you Father?
THE BOSS:	Marcus, Lucy is right. (PAUSE) He is a big part of this company.
THE WIFE:	He really is a nice boy, I like him.
THE SON:	Why is everyone singing his praises? What does he know about anything?
THE DAUGHTER:	Marcus, why don't you like him? Explain to me why you don't.
THE SON:	Lucy, to tell you the truth, it's his arrogance; alongside, him being hell bent on trying to impress everyone with his intelligence and charm.
THE DAUGHTER:	What's wrong with that?
THE SON:	Lucy, you know nothing about him, except for brief meetings when you have come down to the office. Did you know he disappears at a drop of a hat, when he gets a phone call? I have been watching him lately, there is something there. During the meeting we had last week, he got a phone call and got up and left. He's hardly in the office these days and I really don't know how he managed to pull this presentation together without being in the office. Something is wrong, I can feel it.

THE DAUGHTER:	Why do you assume the worst, Marcus? Maybe he has other commitments we don't know about.
THE BOSS:	Now that you have mentioned it, maybe your right? He does get up and go when he gets a certain phone call.
THE SON:	So you have noticed this Father? Isn't that a bit weird? Maybe he's got a deep dark secret that he is hiding from us all?
THE WIFE:	Somehow I don't think so. He really doesn't seem the type.
THE BOSS:	Perhaps he has a love interest?
THE WIFE:	Yes, he probably has, a good-looking boy like him.
THE SON:	May be we should spy on him and see what he is up to?
THE DAUGHTER:	Really Marcus! (PAUSE) You are too much.
THE SON:	I reckon he's seeing that Cynthia, the pretty girl from the office…every time he has a phone call, he goes straight up to her and whispers in her ear and then leaves.
THE WIFE:	Marcus, you might be right. She could be his partner in crime, you never know these days…
THE DAUGHTER:	I think your minds are working overtime. Cynthia, really, have you even seen her Marcus? I mean, close up, really don't make me laugh.
THE SON:	They could be on a mission together, up to something, the pair of them.
THE BOSS:	You know they are quite close. I have seen them myself and another thing…

THE SON:	I think I know what you are thinking Father, have you heard her also?
THE BOSS:	Yes I have. When we have walked past her, she is quickly on the phone.
THE SON:	(RAISED VOICE) They have left the building!
THE WIFE:	Oh really?
THE DAUGHTER:	I really can't believe (PAUSE)…what I am hearing.
THE SON:	Really Lucy! I can see it all now, he is hiding something.
THE BOSS:	Actually, Lucy, come to think of it, Bradley is a lot like you.
THE DAUGHTER:	What do you mean Marcus?
THE SON:	You're a bit mysterious to where you are. We hardly see you.
THE DAUGHTER:	After all that, that's the comparison you come up with? (LAUGHS)
THE SON:	I am only teasing you Lucy, but how comes you are so busy? We used to see a lot more of you before, what's happened?
THE DAUGHTER:	You know how it is, when you got your own place, there is always something to do.
THE SON:	Lucy, all you have to do is ask if you need anything but you've even stopped asking. I take it everything's going okay?
THE DAUGHTER:	Thanks Marcus, it is.
THE BOSS:	Let's go out tonight, to celebrate today's success?
THE SON:	That's a great idea, how about it Lucy?
THE DAUGHTER:	You guys carry on. I've got a prior engagement.
THE WIFE:	Can't you re-arrange it Lucy? It would be nice if you can join us.

THE BOSS:	Perhaps another time then Lucy.
THE DAUGHTER:	Father, Mother, I have to go. I will try and make time, Marcus…
THE SON:	It's always lovely to see you Lucy.
THE DAUGHTER:	Bye! (PECK KISSING AND FOOTSTEPS)
THE SON:	You know Father, maybe we should ask Bradley. (PAUSE) That's if he's not on another mission…with Cynthia (OUTBURSTS OF LAUGHTER)

FADE

Scene 3

**ROMANTIC MUSIC PLAYING IN THE
BACKGROUND. GLASSES
CLINKING TOGETHER. FADE IN ON LAUGHTER
AND CHATTER.**

The daughter at the offices, in the PA's room.

THE PA: (V.O.) Really, you should have seen his face, it was a picture.

THE DAUGHTER: Bradley, you are wicked, winding Marcus up like that.

THE PA: And then he turned up with the quotations, (LAUGHING)

THE DAUGHTER: He was up all night. That's why he was cranky this afternoon, when I met him at the house.

THE PA: The meeting was a success and the presentation great.

THE DAUGHTER: You did work really hard on that Bradley, well done my darling.

THE PA: Thank you!

THE DAUGHTER: I do have other concerns though.

THE PA: What's wrong Lucy, are you okay? It's okay Lucy. I know you tried to tell them.

THE DAUGHTER: If I could have just told Father, it wouldn't have been so bad.

THE PA: I am sure Marcus will come around. (PAUSE) He can't dislike me that much…

THE DAUGHTER:	I have my doubts. He doesn't seem too keen on you and they all are starting to suspect something is up.
THE PA:	What do you mean?
THE DAUGHTER:	They know something's wrong, (PAUSE). That Cynthia's not very good is she?
THE PA:	Listen, I have to let her know that I am coming to see you. Let me know if they leave the office.
THE DAUGHTER:	That's all very well, but they think something's going on between you both, especially when you go up to her and whisper in her ear.
THE PA:	Yes but you know that's not true (SIPPING FROM GLASS). Lucy don't worry about it. I am sure Marcus is not that bad and once he knows, he will welcome me with open arms.
THE DAUGHTER:	Bradley, I hope so but I have a feeling it might get a bit ugly. He is quite upset with you, at the moment, after what happened this morning. He still had nothing good to say about you this afternoon—"golden boy", as he puts it.
THE PA:	(CLOSE) Lucy, you know what you mean to me.
THE DAUGHTER:	I know, but you know what it's been like for us since you have joined the company.
THE PA:	You know something Lucy, we have to tell them. Let's do it together.
THE DAUGHTER:	Bradley, no, I don't think that's a good idea.
THE PA:	But why?

THE DAUGHTER:	I don't know how Marcus would react to seeing us together.
THE PA:	He's going to find out sooner or later.
THE DAUGHTER:	Tell you the truth, I'd rather it is later.

FADE IN ON GLASSES BEING REFILLED.

THE DAUGHTER:	Just half a glass for me, thank you my love.
THE PA:	I do have a suggestion…
THE DAUGHTER:	What do you suggest?
THE PA:	How about if we both approach your parents, tell them first and then take Marcus on because then we will have your parents blessing and their back up.
THE DAUGHTER:	You know, (PAUSE) Bradley, that does seem like a good idea.
THE PA:	I don't want you getting upset. I don't like it.
THE DAUGHTER:	Feeling much happier at this thought. Father will be pleased. He does like you—

FADE IN ON BUZZER, INTERCOM. FIRM FEMALE VOICE.

FEMALE VOICE:	(D) Mr Harris, Senior Mr Jenkins has called a meeting, asap, in his office.
THE PA:	(D) Thank you, Mrs Brue.
THE DAUGHTER:	Father's here, it must be important.
THE PA:	Lucy, (PAUSE) after the meeting we can tell him.
THE DAUGHTER:	Only if Mother's here also, let's go and see…

**ROMANTIC MUSIC MUTED. GLASSES CLANGING
ON THE TABLE.
FADE IN ON DOOR OPENING AND CLOSING.**

THE BOSS:	Ahh, Bradley, Lucy, glad you're both here. Come in, pull up a chair. (SLIDING CHAIR)
THE WIFE:	Lucy, you wanted to tell us your good news? You were saying earlier?
THE DAUGHTER:	It can wait Father, you called a meeting? Everything okay?
THE BOSS:	Marcus is on his way, we'll just wait for him…
THE WIFE:	You sure Lucy, you can tell us. (PAUSE) Keeping us waiting in the dark?
THE DAUGHTER:	Mother, I am so happy today.
THE BOSS:	That's good to hear Lucy. You are doing well for yourself. You've finished your degree; you set your own standards at the company and you've got a beautiful place here. What more could a girl want?
THE WIFE:	All you need now is someone to share it with.
THE DAUGHTER:	On that note, talking about sharing, I have been seeing someone.
THE BOSS:	Oh Lucy, that's great news – wait, is it serious?
THE DAUGHTER:	Put it this way Father, if he will have me, you're looking at a potential son-in-law…
THE WIFE:	What? Wedding bells? Lucy, you have kept this quiet, when? I mean, how long have you been seeing him?
THE BOSS:	Lucy, now you know what kind of man he should be, don't you? He

	can't be just anybody! But there again, if you are happy then…
THE WIFE:	I think I'm going to cry, I'm so happy for you—
THE DAUGHTER:	We have been seeing each other for a while now, about three years.
THE BOSS:	Three years? How can that be? You're either at the office working hard, at ours, or at your place, but we haven't seen anyone come or go?
THE WIFE:	Lucy, three years? (PAUSE) Oh how marvellous!
THE BOSS:	What's his name and what does he do?
THE WIFE:	John, really, let Lucy tell us.
THE DAUGHTER:	Well, I think you can ask him yourself…
THE PA:	Mr and Mrs Jenkins, how are you both?
THE BOSS:	What? Bradley?
THE WIFE:	Oh my goodness, you have been seeing Lucy all this time?
THE BOSS:	Now it makes sense…you didn't need to leave the office at all.
THE WIFE:	Cynthia was a cover up; oh you two are really wicked. We thought Cynthia was your love interest. (GIGGLING)
THE BOSS:	You know, Bradley, there were times when I had my suspicions. I did think that there might be something between you both, but then I just dismissed it.
THE PA:	Did you? Why did you dismiss the thought?
THE BOSS:	Well I wasn't hundred percent sure, just at times I had my doubts.
THE PA:	In what way?

THE BOSS:	Oh, just the way you looked at Lucy at times.
THE DAUGHTER:	Father, Mother, this is Bradley, the love of my life.
THE BOSS:	Come here son. (PAUSE) Welcome to the family.
THE WIFE:	Bradley, Bradley, all this time, I didn't have a clue.
THE PA:	I'm sorry about not telling you, but we just wanted to be sure that this is what we both wanted.
THE WIFE:	I have to say, I didn't suspect anything at all but Bradley I am glad it's you.
THE PA:	Thank you Mrs Jenkins.
THE BOSS:	I am so happy for you Lucy. I don't think I could ask for a better son-in-law.
THE PA:	Mr Jenkins, my apologies again for keeping this under wraps.
THE DAUGHTER:	Father it's okay, isn't it?
THE BOSS:	Lucy, it's okay and it's also time to celebrate.
THE WIFE:	Yes of course, perhaps this evening Lucy? We can celebrate at home?
THE PA:	Lucy, are you feeling happy?
THE DAUGHTER:	Bradley, thank you so much.
THE BOSS:	You know Bradley, I have been thinking quite a bit lately about myself and the company.
THE PA:	Mr Jenkins, that is up to you how you choose to do things.
THE BOSS:	Bradley, please, you can call me, Dad. I think you have just made things clearer to me.
THE DAUGHTER:	Father don't make any hasty decisions, but be sure this is what you want.

THE WIFE:	Lucy, I think what your father is trying to say is that now it's different, knowing that Bradley will be a part of this family also…
THE BOSS:	Have you too thought of a date yet?
THE PA:	Yes, we are looking towards the end of this year.
THE DAUGHTER:	Autumn, it's so wonderful when the leaves fall off the trees. I would like a wedding at around about that time.
THE BOSS:	This is perfect timing. I need to draw up the paper and put my proposal forward to my chosen successor. Then we have got a wedding to organise.
THE WIFE:	I am so excited. Everyone is going to be so happy for you Lucy. You are both lucky to have found each other this way.
THE PA:	Thank you both, but I think we are forgetting someone important.
THE BOSS:	I think the most important people are all here.
THE WIFE:	John, Bradley is right.
THE PA:	Marcus…
THE DAUGHTER:	Oh Father, Marcus, he will be upset.
THE BOSS:	Oh dear, how could I forget about Marcus?
THE WIFE:	Lucy, I think there might be a slight problem, as your father has also chosen a successor.
THE DAUGHTER:	Have you Father?
THE BOSS:	Bradley…Lucy don't worry about anything, just enjoy this moment.
THE PA:	Dad, thank you very much.
THE WIFE:	John, you have made the right choice…
THE DAUGHTER:	What do you mean, Mother?

THE BOSS: Bradley, welcome to our family and
to your company...

FADE

Scene 4

**FADE IN ON FOOTSTEPS. CHAIRS PULLED UP.
CORK POPPING.**

Back at the family home, the boss, the wife and the son.

THE SON:	I was nearly there Father, had to come back. What happened?
THE BOSS:	Sorry son, this couldn't wait. Bradley's bringing Lucy back.
THE WIFE:	We have some good news for you and there is more…
THE SON:	That's good, but I could have brought Lucy back home. I am sure "golden boy" has work to do.
THE BOSS:	Once they're here son, I will explain everything. Perhaps a glass of champagne while we wait?
THE SON:	What's the occasion?

**FADE UP ON DOORBELL. OPENING AND CLOSING
DOOR. HUSTLE OF FOOTSTEPS. LOUD CHATTER.**

THE DAUGHTER:	Marcus, so glad that you're here.
THE SON:	Hello Lucy…Oh! Bradley.
THE PA:	Marcus, you okay from this morning?
THE SON:	Why wouldn't I be?
THE PA:	It's been a long day, that's all was asking…

THE BOSS:	Marcus, listen carefully! I have something to tell you.
THE SON:	If you don't mind Bradley, we are having a private family meeting, so you can go. I am sure you have got lots of things to do…
THE WIFE:	Marcus, don't be so rude.
THE SON:	I don't understand. I have to put up with him at the office and now…at home also?
THE BOSS:	Marcus, calm down! Bradley is here because he's got an announcement to make and so have I—
THE DAUGHTER:	Father, I think you should go first…
THE BOSS:	Okay Lucy, if that's what you want. Marcus, I have made my choice as to who will run the company once I step down. (SOUND OF SOFT COUCH, BEING SAT ON)
THE SON:	Mother, I will have that glass of champagne after all… (POURING SOUND)
THE BOSS:	Bradley is going to take over from me.
THE SON:	(CHAMPAGNE SPILLING OUT OF THE MOUTH) What! You can't be serious?
THE BOSS:	Marcus, I expect you to respect my decision.
THE WIFE:	There is more to this, if you just listen, Marcus.
THE SON:	I have been up all night, had a hectic morning trying to nail that deal. Just when I thought that things couldn't get any worse, you do this to me? Golden boy!
THE DAUGHTER:	Wait! (PAUSE) Father is trying to explain something to you.

THE SON:	What is there to explain? Well, Bradley, congratulations! You got what you wanted, it's all yours. If you are really going ahead with this Father, then I am out. If you think for a minute that I will be working for him…then you are truly mistaken.
THE BOSS:	Marcus, there is a reason why I have chosen Bradley.
THE SON:	Father, you have made your choice and it's not fine with me. I just can't believe what I am hearing—
THE DAUGHTER:	Mother, I think that it's best that we leave.
THE WIFE:	Lucy, I think you need to tell Marcus.
THE DAUGHTER:	I don't think it's the right time, perhaps another time.
THE PA:	Perhaps we should both leave.
THE SON:	(ANGRY VOICE) Wait! (PAUSE) What do you mean…you should both leave? Lucy is staying – you should leave, golden boy.
THE DAUGHTER:	This is not how it's supposed to be, it's all wrong.
THE BOSS:	Lucy, please don't get upset, it's a day of celebration.
THE WIFE:	Marcus you're not listening, okay you might be a little upset—
THE SON:	Upset? Really Mother, that's an understatement. I think we should talk once Bradley has left.
THE DAUGHTER:	Bradley is not going anywhere. If I'm staying, so is he.
THE PA:	Lucy, I think it's best that I go for now.
THE SON:	Am I missing something here?

| THE BOSS: | Maybe you're right, we'll have to leave this until he's has had a chance to calm down. |
| THE SON: | Leave what? No I want to hear this…what's going on? |

FADE IN ON FOOTSTEPS. DOOR OPENING AND CLOSING. COATS RUFFLING. WHISPERING.

THE WIFE:	Lucy will call you later okay?
THE BOSS:	(LOW) Please don't worry, everything will be okay.
THE PA:	It's best, all round, to leave it for now.
THE DAUGHTER:	You can't even talk to him, when he's like this. (STARTS TO CRY)
THE PA:	(CLOSE) Come here… (HUGS LUCY)
THE DAUGHTER:	I thought we'll have a double celebration tonight, but that's not going to happen.
THE PA:	It's okay, don't upset yourself and hush. (KISSES LUCY ON THE FOREHEAD)
THE WIFE:	(LOW) Once he hears your father out completely, he will understand.

FADE IN ON DOOR SLAMMING SHUT. FOOTSTEPS RUNNING TOWARDS THE READER.

THE SON:	(OFF) Take your hands off my sister, how dare you!
THE PA:	No! Marcus it's not what you think…
THE BOSS:	We can explain, listen—
THE SON:	Who do you think you are? I am here to comfort my sister, don't need you.

THE WIFE:	If you just let your father explain, Marcus, then—
THE DAUGHTER:	No, he was just…Marcus it's not how it looks but—

FADE UP ON LOUD PUNCH.

THE DAUGHTER:	(CLOSE) No…
THE PA:	Marcus, get off me!
THE SON:	You think you can put your hands on my sister? Do you?
THE PA:	That hurt! Listen Marcus, back off or else—
THE SON:	Or else? Is that a threat?
THE WIFE:	How can you hit Bradley, Marcus? Stop this at once, let go of him.
THE BOSS:	Right, that's it, come here. (DRAGGING SOUND)
THE DAUGHTER:	Are you okay Bradley?
THE PA:	I am fine. I could retaliate, but Lucy, I know he's your brother.
THE SON:	(OFF) All you care about is him! (BEING USHERED AWAY)
THE DAUGHTER:	Marcus, I love Bradley and we are going to get married…
THE BOSS:	(STOPS IN HIS TRACKS) Lucy…
THE SON:	What did you just say? Did I hear you right?

FADE UP ON SLOW FOOTSTEPS.

THE PA:	Bradley, I erm…
THE SON:	No, you shut up, not talking to you.
THE BOSS:	This is Lucy's good news.
THE SON:	Wait…you both knew about this? How long has this been going on?
THE DAUGHTER:	We didn't want to tell you like this, please.

THE WIFE:	Let's go and sit down and talk about this…Bradley are you okay?
THE BOSS:	As Bradley will be taking over the company, I suggest—
THE SON:	So let me get this right. Everyone knew, except me. Bradley, what can I say…you have hit the jackpot, hey? So that's why you're taking over, golden boy, because you're with my sister! You have done well for yourself. (PATTING ON THE BACK)
THE DAUGHTER:	Letting Bradley takeover was Father's decision and it was made before they knew about us.
THE SON:	You expect me to believe that? Why would Father favour him over me?
THE BOSS:	If you listen, then I will explain. I chose Bradley because he is my right-hand man, more experienced than you. He would run it until the end of the year, in the process you learn from him and then you take over, that is the plan. Also, at the end of the year, your sister's planning to get married!
THE SON:	You expect me to just lie down and roll over?
THE WIFE:	Give him a chance, he's not that bad.
THE SON:	No wonder you got your back up earlier when we spoke about Cynthia. So it wasn't Cynthia after all.
THE BOSS:	You feeling a bit better now? You calmed down now?
THE PA:	I want Lucy to be happy and to be honest I don't want to come between

	you and your brother. I know how much you care and love him.
THE SON:	What, you'd walk away if you had to? Just like that?
THE PA:	I thought it was just banter between us, but punching me is going too far. As for Lucy, Marcus, I love your sister very much. You want me to walk away from the company, that's fine, but I won't walk away from your sister. I am going to marry her, that's if she'll have me. I'll make her happy; she is the love of my life. I don't want to fight with you anymore more, okay…?
THE SON:	My sister's really had an effect on you, never knew you had a nice side to you. Well it looks like golden boy has got himself a golden girl…Lucy I am happy for you okay.
THE WIFE:	Oh Marcus, thank you.
THE BOSS:	Where's that champagne? Celebrations after all…
THE SON:	Sorry about your face, Bradley, you know Lucy means the world to me too.
THE PA:	So that means you're okay with us?
THE SON:	I will be watching you. If you hurt my sister in any way! Besides, I'll have to put up with you forever now – just great!
THE DAUGHTER:	Thank you, this means a lot to me.
THE PA:	Come here, Marcus…
THE SON:	No, it's okay, you can save the hugs for my sister. (ALL LAUGH)

END